# Praise For High School Here I come _____

"This book not only talked about academics but also our future social lives and potential oppositions and challenges. 10/10 I'm not as nervous about high school anymore." KIK

"A must-read for your teen. This book is a valuable resource that helped my teen navigate the stresses and the pressure that high school can potentially bring. It taught my daughter resiliency skills lovingly and compassionately." GH

"*High School Here I Come* gave me a good idea about high school and what to expect. It opened my eyes and helped me to prepare for what is coming in high school. I am still a little scared about high school, but I feel better prepared. It was a good book; it helped me feel better about going to high school: I feel calmer and more relaxed when thinking about starting high school." AJB

"I wish everyone would benefit from reading this book. I love it. It makes you aware of potential and less stressed about the future. I felt safe and gained awareness. This book helped me a lot. It made me love myself again, and believe in myself going forward into the future." CC

"By reading this book, I was able to think about what I would and wouldn't do in certain conditions. The activities allowed me to learn a lot about myself, and I got an idea of what high school is like." IH

"I feel so much better about myself. I learned a lot from this book. It taught me to have strength and faith in myself. Sometimes things are going to be challenging. It made me feel more confident and less scared for high school." GC

"I am more confident and less stressed. This book taught me how to react in different situations. It taught me a lot and opened my mind. I learned how to relieve stress and build my self-esteem. This book also taught me how to overcome stressful situations in high school.
It was beneficial." YF

"I thought this book was beneficial. It gave me different aspects of high school. It gave me the importance of staying true to myself." SB

# High School Here I Come:
# Preparing for the Journey

———————————————

**Marcella Penny Kowalchuk**

Library of Congress Cataloging-in-Publication Data

**Kowalchuk, Marcella Penny**

High School Here I Come - Preparing for the journey \

Marcella Penny Kowalchuk

Juvenile Nonfiction > Social Issues > Adolescence

Juvenile Nonfiction > Social Issues > Self-Esteem & Self-Reliance

978-1-990461-07-1

LLH Publishing House

1st Printing: September 2021. Printed in Canada

Cover Photo Credit: Marcus N. Carasco  MNPhoto Studio

Illustrator: Jade Brown

Editor: Lindy Bailey

**Publisher's Note & Author DISCLAIMER**

This publication is designed to provide accurate and authoritative information concerning the subject matter covered. It is sold to understand that the publisher and author are not engaging in or rendering any psychological, medical, or other professional services. If expert assistance or counselling is needed, seek the services of a competent medical professional. The information included in this guide is accurate at the time of publication. The views and opinions expressed in the YouTube links are those of the speakers and not those of the author, Marcella Kowalchuk Consulting Incorporated or the Publisher. For immediate support, call your local crisis line. Be Well.

# Dedication

---

To mom, thank you for your love. You are the most beautiful, wise, funny and kind woman I know.

# TABLE OF CONTENTS:

**HIGH SCHOOL: THE NEW FRONTIER**

- THE HIGH SCHOOL ENVIRONMENT: *THINGS ARE SO DIFFERENT*
- GETTING TO SCHOOL: *HOW AM I GOING TO GET THERE?*
- THE BUILDING: *WHERE IS THE MAP?*
- STUDENT POPULATION: *HOW MANY PEOPLE GO HERE?*
- CLASSES, COURSES AND CREDITS: *HOW DO I CHOOSE?*
- THE ACADEMIC YEAR: *QUADMESTER? SEMESTER? WHAT?*
- GETTING GOOD GRADES: *HOW DO I PULL THIS OFF?*
- **ACTIVITY THREE:** LIST THE WAYS YOU PROCRASTINATE
- IT'S NOT ALL ABOUT THE WORK: *YOU MEAN I CAN HAVE FUN TOO?*
- KEY TAKEAWAY

**FRIENDSHIPS: PAST PRESENT AND FUTURE**

- THE COURSE OF FRIENDSHIPS: *WHO'S COMING AND GOING?*
- FRIENDSHIPS: *HOW TO MAKE EM?*

# Introduction:

---

## Introduction:

---

## The Pimple Catastrophe: Experimentation Gone Awry.

On a warm September morning, I stood waiting for the school bus. I was dressed in my uniform white shirt neatly ironed, tucked into my kilt, kneehigh socks and blue suede shoes. I avoided the standard black because blue was my favourite colour, and the school was not such a stickler on shoe colour then. My natural hair was chemically relaxed, and my skinny brown legs appear slimmer and longer under the itchy woollen kilt, which I rolled up at the waist to shorten its length.

Waiting for the bus, thinking nervously about what high school would be like, I felt excited and scared. I also had a tingling feeling on the left side of my face, just under my eye on my upper cheek. Well, it was more than a tingle; it was more of a sting. You see, I was prone to breakouts and had pimples. In the weeks leading up to the beginning of high school, there seemed to be an explosion of pimples

1

on my face. I decided to take the situation into my own hands. To manage this pimple catastrophe, I devised a plan to rid myself of this problem.

Knowing the importance of starting small with any experiment, I focused on the most offensive culprit to destroy. I searched our bathroom cupboard and found a disinfecting solution commonly used in our household to clean and sanitize surface areas. I diluted a small amount of this cleaner and proceeded to use it to kill the pimple. I would use a cotton ball twice a day to dab the "pimple-killing solution" on my face. It stung every time I did it, but in my mind, this meant that it was doing the job.

By the time the first school day came in September, the solution had gotten rid of the pimple. One down, but a whole face still to go. Sheesh!!!! I did not realize that the solution was a harmful skin irritant and caused damage to the area like a burn. The disinfecting solution had a skull and crossbones symbol, which should have been my first indication to stay away. However, I had a greater priority: looking good and fabulous for high school.

All the other preparation activities of buying books and supplies and choosing my classes were not as important as fitting in and being popular. Being liked and popular was one of my biggest concerns at the time, not my grades.

# High School Here I Come Preparing for the Journey.

I wrote this book because the transition to high school can cause excitement, nervousness, anxiety and joy. You may be wondering how things will be different and what may stay the same. You may even wonder how you will change.

To help you prepare for this journey, the central chapters of this book focus on five areas, all connected to you, and they include Your Family, The School and Academic Environment, Friendships, Your Well-Being and Safety, and most importantly, Being True to You. Within each chapter, the sections identify topics of interest specific to girls beginning their high school journey. As you read, there are activities for you to capture your thoughts and reflect upon your feelings as they relate to each section. I hope you find this book helpful, and after reading it, feel more prepared, less anxious, and excited to make the most of your high school experience. Are you ready? Let's begin.

**You at This Moment:** What Will High School Be Like?

When you think about what your high school experience will be like, what is the immediate sensation you feel? Is it fear, excitement, joy, hope? Do you look forward to this time in your life with an expectation of wonder and freedom? Do you see this as a chance to become more independent, more responsible and make new friends? Or do you cringe? Are you worried about fitting in? Do you wonder if you are smart enough, whether you will be able to find your class and have someone to sit with at lunch? Aghhhhhh. How do you think things may change for you?

Take a few minutes to think about these feelings and write them down.

# Activity #1

---

Reflect on your thoughts of how you feel about going to high school.

**Write Your Thoughts:**

Looking at your list, what do you believe has influenced your feelings about high school?

Media (movies, songs, television shows, social networking sites) friends and family can and in many ways has led to how you think and feel about the high school experience. High school is an essential part of one's identity and is the unifying time for developing lifelong friendships. **Write Your Thoughts:**

# Key Takeaway

---

High school is a time of change and transition. This time can cause feelings of excitement, fear and confusion as you wonder what this time will be like and who you are in this new reality. Your parents, friends, family, and society all may have certain expectations of you. And these expectations may sometimes make you feel overwhelmed. In fact, at times, being overwhelmed is an accurate description of the pressure you may feel. By thoughtfully addressing and reflecting on how you feel and think about your relationships, wellbeing, and goals, I hope you can prepare as best as you can for the journey ahead.

# Family Expectations, Hopes and Dreams

_____

# Family Expectations, Hopes and Dreams

Your parents and family have very particular expectations and hopes for you. They want you to remember and practice the lessons they have taught you through the years. They want you to make good choices and do well, and they want you to make them proud.

## Time for the "Talk": *Oh Boy!!!!*

If you have not already, you may begin to have crucial conversations with parents and individual family members about preparing for high school. I like to refer to conversations as the "Talk." This talk can be given in a private one-to-one chat with a family member, or it can be given to you less formally in every discussion about family life. Often, the adult will share their experience through stories focused on the good, the bad, and the funny aspects of high school. It may usually end with a loving command to study hard and get good

11

grades. You may also receive a stern warning not to let others distract you from your schoolwork and do what is right.

# Your Family's Hopes and Dreams for You: *No Pressure*

You will be told about the importance of your marks, as they will influence your ability to go to college or university and your ability to have a great future. You may also be reminded that going to school for many girls in other countries is a privilege, and some even risk their lives to attend school. All of this is true.

Because of the love your parents and family have for you and their responsibility to care for and protect you, they will want you to be safe, happy and have a promising future. Therefore, the "Talk" will also include information about girls' difficulties during their high school years. Your family (as well as other adults) will tell you about society's pressure on girls to conform to a certain standard of beauty. Girls are often asked to adjust themselves to make others happy. You will be warned about bullies and will also be reminded to stand up for what is right.

Most of all, your family will let you know how proud they are of you. As you prepare for high school, they will share their hopes and dreams for you; that you get to learn new things, make new friends, explore your interests, build your confidence and change and work towards your future goals.

# Hold On to Your Family Values: *What Does That Even Mean?*

High school will be one of the first occasions where you will encounter new people and make friends without connecting to them through your parents and family. This increased level of autonomy will allow you to decide who you spend your time with, what you spend your time doing and how you act.

Your family will expect you to be trusted to act according to the values and cultural practices they taught you: be kind, truthful, honest, and respect yourself and others. They understand that you will have disappointments, successes, make mistakes, and learn from those mistakes. They also know that high school will provide you with experiences to learn, grow and enjoy the wonderful opportunities that will come your way.

Sometimes your family may seem strict, and at times there may be disagreements about what you want and what your family wants for you. Remember that your family has your best interest in mind. Though you may have clashes over your clothes, music, how you want to express yourself, your grades and even some of your friends; this is part of growing up. There will be times when you and your parents may disagree on the choices you are making. When such times occur, remember that they will hurt when you hurt and that they want what is best for you.

Your family will expect you not to forget the values of their culture and beliefs as you mature. Do not forget their love for you, even when you believe they are being over-protective or think they are out of touch and too strict.

# Activity #2

---

**Reflect on the expectations of family members.**

- What are some of the lessons your family has shared with you in the "Talk"?
- What are some of the ways your family shows you their love for you?
- How do your family members speak about their high school experience?
- What values does your family want you to uphold?

**Write Your Thoughts:**

# Key Takeaway

_____

As you learn new lessons, make new friends, have new experiences and are being exposed to other ideas, your relationships with your parents and family may change. The love and support of your family will serve as the foundation for how you have experienced life so far. As you continue through your high school journey, remember that your family has great hopes for your success and they dream of you growing up and going into the world to do great things.

# High School: The New Frontier

---

# High School – The New Frontier

---

## The High School Environment: *Things Are So Different*

The high school experience will be quite different from elementary school in a few ways. Let us consider some of the apparent differences between your elementary school and high school.

## Getting to School: *How Am I Going to Get There?*

Your elementary school was most likely in your neighbourhood. In kindergarten, you may have been dropped off or walked with an adult. As you grew older, you may have walked to school on your own or with friends. There was often a crossing guard to help as you crossed the street, and teachers stood outside your school to welcome you to class.

Getting to your new high school might require you to travel another path. If your high school is still walking distance from your home, you are probably already familiar with the route to get there. You and your friends may have planned where you will meet up to make your way there together.

If you are new to the neighbourhood or do not live close to your high school, you may still be required to make your way without the assistance of your parents or a crossing guard. You may be required to take the bus, subway, train, or a combination of various modes of transportation.

To prepare to arrive at school on time, you will need to be familiar with the safest way to get to school. You will also need to learn alternate safe routes. Discovering these other routes can be great fun as you explore different paths, which you can select based on the season, time it takes to get you to class, what is nearby and who or what you may encounter along the way.

To find alternate routes, you can spend some time in the weeks before you begin high school learning the bus routes and schedules, the different walking paths, and talking with your friends about getting to school on time. Getting to and from school provides an excellent opportunity to chat with your friends and meet new ones while you share stories about interesting things. For a moment, imagine you and your friends walking home after school laughing and joking around while you talk about the experiences of the day. Doesn't it sound like fun?

# The Building: *Where Is the Map?*

When you think about your elementary school building now, it can appear small and quite familiar. If you have attended the same school since kindergarten, you may be so used to the building that you know every hallway, classroom, and washroom location and could easily find your friends on the playground. Your elementary school might have had only a main floor, a small gym and a lunch area.

Your new high school building might be multilevelled with a large gym, classrooms in the main building, portables on the grounds, plus a football field. Classrooms will be set up based on the courses taught in those rooms (Information Technology, Construction & Design, Art, Science, Geography, Cosmetology, etc.).

Instead of a cubby or hook for hanging your jacket and school bag, you may have assigned lockers. Attending classes will require you to navigate between hallways, floors and portables as well as accessing different building entry and exit points.

Though you might initially be overwhelmed by the size and layout of your high school, learning how to get around is something that you will figure out. Some sections may be occupied by certain groups of students based on cliques, age, grade, music, fashion style and social club preferences.

It may take you a few minutes to get from one class to the other, and there may be instances in the beginning when you may get lost or find yourself in the wrong class or area. But this will get better over time. One thing is for sure; you will not be the first student who has walked into the wrong class, nor the last. If this happens, you have a choice; you can get up and leave or stay and excuse yourself to go to the bathroom and not return. Once out of the class, you can figure out where you should be by asking a teacher or another student. When you finally get to class, you will be a few minutes late, but that's OK; such experiences are expected. Brush it off and move on.

Before the school year starts, schools give tours to new students to help them find their way around, which is time well spent. It can also be an excellent opportunity to meet other students and bond over this experience. If you have an older sibling or relative that goes to high school, you can ask them to show you around. (Note: They may charge you for this favour.)

# Student Population: *How Many People Go Here?*

The student population is going to be very different from elementary school, whereas you are leaving a school where you were part of the oldest age group and you will now be part of the youngest age category in your first year of high school. As part of the new incoming freshman class, you will be joining a new social environment of great variety based on the number of students, their age, size, cultural background, gender, personal expression, academic knowledge, physical ability, social, economic class, religious/faith belief, family configuration, personal experiences and school tenure.

Whether you attend an all-girls school, mixed or private school, students always find ways to separate and differentiate their styles. Defining your uniqueness is expected at this stage, and you will notice that many other students strive to be unique but dress like their friends.

Though you will be a new face in the crowd, you can be sure that an entire group of other new faces may be feeling the same as you. Embrace the experience, be friendly to others and know that you are now a part of this variety of the student body.

# Classes, Courses and Credits: *How Do I Choose?*

Most of your classes may have been in the same classroom in elementary school except for gym and music. Based on your grade, you may have had the same teacher for Reading, Writing, Math, English,

Social Studies, History, Health and Physical Education.

High school provides you with the opportunity to take many different courses as you advance through your years. Each class will have a diverse group of students and another teacher. You will be able to work in groups for projects, join different school clubs based on Arts, Technology, Science, Sports, and so much more.

Students must pass credit courses that include mandatory and elective subjects to graduate. Before each term begins, you will need to decide which classes you are taking and what level. Some high schools offer courses taught at different levels, such as General, Advanced Placement, Academic Pathway, Open, Alternative or College preparation. These course types are geared towards what pathway you may want to take after high school. While you may start in a particular course type, you can make changes to suit your needs better. Teaching lessons can include inperson or remote learning, using various technology and tools depending on the class structure.

Choose courses that are of interest to you and give you the credits you need to graduate from high school. Though you may not like all the mandatory courses you have to take through the years, you will have various elective courses to explore your interests.

You will also learn that teachers have different teaching styles and expectations for how your work is to be completed. It is essential to pay attention in class to understand your teachers' requirements. An additional requirement in high school is participating in activities that serve the community through volunteer hours. These experiences are a fantastic way to learn more about the community and its needs and make the world a better place.

You can seek the guidance of your parents, family, or teachers to help you decide about your course and talk to others about the classes you are interested in taking.

Before the school year begins, you can also attend the orientation to learn and ask questions about the courses and supports available.

# The Academic Year:
## *Quadmester? Semester? What?*

One aspect of high school, which may take you by surprise is the course curriculum and timetable. Your year will be divided into semesters, terms or quadmesters. A year split into quadmesters is when students take two courses at a time across four separate academic semesters. A year split into semesters is when students are enrolled in four classes at a time across two separate academic semesters. You will have a set time to complete your credit courses during the academic year to pass each grade and advance towards graduation. (Remember, this is the goal.)

There will be group projects, individual assignments, tests, and final exams for which you will be responsible throughout the academic year. Determining if you have learned the course material, applying the lessons, and managing your time and schedule are the reasons for these exercises.

With each semester, you will become more familiar with the flow of the academic year. You will learn to select your courses and arrange your schedule to handle your schoolwork with other activities you are interested in, such as team sports, clubs, or part-time jobs. And with the options of online learning, summer classes and coop experiences, the opportunity for you to learn and complete course work in non-traditional ways can be exciting.

## Getting Good Grades: *How Do I Pull This Off?*

Getting good grades is essential; however, they are not you. Your marks will reflect the effort you put into the work assigned to you and how well you prepared and understood the lesson. You will be required to be more independent and manage your time to get good grades. In elementary school, your teacher may have walked around the class, looking over your shoulder to see if you were doing your work correctly.

When you are in high school, you cannot wait or depend on your teacher to ask you if you need help or understand the lesson. Support is available, and you will have to take the initiative and be responsible to seek and ask for help.

Like most things in life, you can prepare to get good grades by applying tips that others have used before you. A few are listed below for you, and there is space for you to add others:

- Get to class on time and pay attention while you are in class.
- Know when your assignments and test are due
- If you do not understand the lesson, say so.
- Ask for help from your teacher, guidance counsellor as tutors and after school help is available.
- The sooner you ask for help, the better.
- At home, set up a place just for you to do your work free from distractions.
- Set a specific time to do your work and complete assignments.
- Turn off any devices with notifications that can easily pull your attention from your work.
- Get a good night's sleep.

- Schedule time to work with a friend to make it more fun and share what you both know.
- Be aware of how and why you procrastinate.

# Activity #3

**Reflection:**

In section **A**, list the ways you procrastinate, and in section **B,** list the reasons why.

**Section A - Ways I procrastinate:**

- 
- 
- 
- 
- 
- 
- 

**Section B - The reasons why I procrastinate:**

- 
- 
- 
- 
- 
- 
-

Now that you have thought about how you procrastinate, recognize it when it happens the next time you do so. Smile at yourself, and then get on with your schoolwork!

## More Than Just the Grades: *You Mean We Can Have Fun Too?*

The amount of fun you have in high school will depend on you. There are so many enjoyable extracurricular activities that you can get involved with to meet other students, develop your talents, learn new skills or just try something new. There are school dances, afterschool clubs and opportunities to compete against other schools in team sports. In addition to arts, drama and music, you can participate in science, math and design competitions. Even better, some teachers are committed to giving their time to help students who want to learn a new skill or participate in an afterschool club. There are also opportunities for you to start your club of interest. You may also be amazed to find out that what interests you also interests someone else.

You will be able to be bold and try out for different teams and offered activities. These are called tryouts for a reason and can help build your confidence and encourage you to pursue new activities.

There is also the simple pleasure of just hanging out with your friends, going to the movies, spending time meeting up with friends from other schools, studying, and so much more.

# Key Takeaway

In high school, teachers, guidance counsellors, and tutoring help are available to you. As high school provides for a more independent learning environment, it is partly your responsibility to raise your hand, speak up and ask for assistance. You are important enough to get the help and support you need. You must share your feelings of being overwhelmed, seriously stressed out and anxious because of your schoolwork with your parents, teachers or counsellors. Conversely, if there is more you want to do at school, let this be known. School is supposed to be a safe place where you are tested within your capabilities, to develop your thinking and problem-solving abilities. Learning and experimenting in your classes can be both challenging and fun.

# Friendships:

# Past, Present and Future

———————————————

# Friendships:

# Past, Present and Future

---

## The Course of Friendships: *Who's Coming and Going*

When you start high school, you may realize that some of the friends you made when you were younger may not go to the same school. The good news is that you can carry on with those friendships and stay in touch if you continue to participate in the same social activities through text, planned visits and online with your parents' permission. And even if your friends go to the same high school as you, you will still make new friends.

You will also notice that your friendships will change and evolve. You may start off having someone you spent a lot of time with in the past, but as you both move towards other interests, you may not connect as often as you used to. But with your new experiences and entering high school, you will be provided with the opportunity to make new friends.

# Friendships: *How Do You Make 'Em?*

Growing up and the high school experience will bring you friends from many different sources. Friendship sources include those from a part-time job, team or club from school, your various classes and volunteering. You will also have the opportunity to meet and make friends if you spend time with family in a different neighbourhood or have moved before starting high school.

When you are about to enter a new environment, you may be worried that you will not make any friends. For some, this is a considerable concern when they start to think about high school. If this is something that you have been thinking about, consider the following suggestions for making friends.

1. Be open to the idea that other students feel the same way you do and are looking to make friends.

2. Say hello when you meet other students. You can meet other students when you are registering for a class, joining a team, waiting in line to get onto the bus, participating in the grade 9 orientation, walking in the halls or when you are shopping for school items.

3. Offer your help if you notice another student looking lost, confused or lonely.

4. Share and compare your schedule with a student next to you to see if you have any classes together.

5. Ask a student to join you at lunch if they are sitting alone.

6. Offer to walk home or ride the bus with a student on the same travel route.

The new friends you will encounter, as well as the friends from your past will be there with you as you get settled into high school life, study for tests, work on assignments, hang out and share this experience of growing up. You will also find that there will be times when there will be friction as you navigate your friendships.

# Disagreements and Squabbles: *He Said, She Said*

There will be times of conflict between you and your friends. You may have arguments about straightforward matters such as what movie to watch or what to put on a pizza. There may also be more serious disputes, such as how you treat each other, whether to cheat on a test or do something that is not appropriate for your age. You must learn how to work out and resolve disagreements and quarrels.

When conflict situations arise, it can be very challenging to sort out among you and your friends. Therefore, you may want to take time to calm down and help your friends do so as well. Consider how important the issue is that you are all dealing with at the moment. Maybe you have time to sit and talk through it right away, or it deserves more time to discuss. There is always the option to leave and walk away.

For other types of disagreements, you may also want to consider whether you can solve the matter independently or need help from a family member or teacher. If the conflict requires you to decide very quickly whether you will participate or act in a way that is against the good values and lessons taught to you by your family, trust your instincts, and follow your values. Doing this may be tricky, as the desire to be liked is powerful, but remember to not act in haste.

# Rethinking This Friendship: *I'm Not Sure about You*

There will be occasions where you question whether you will continue with a friendship. To prepare for this situation, you need to be aware of yourself and your kind of friends and remove yourself from a circumstance that makes you uncomfortable. You might get a sense that you are taking a different path than this group of friends. If you choose to walk away from the situation, you can discuss later with your friends why you decided to leave and not participate in the activity.

After some time, if you decide that you face these types of disagreements more and more with your friends, you may spend less time with this friendship group. The result of this action may be that you may lose these friends, or they will come to see your point of view. Either way, you need to be prepared; this is what growing up and friendship is all about. You cannot put yourself in harm's way and do what is against your values and beliefs for the sake of being liked.

Your friendships will begin to gain increasing importance and greatly influence what you do or do not do, which is why your family will often remind you of the importance of choosing good friends. Whether it is maintaining old friendships or making new ones, you ought to be clear on the standards for the friends you choose.

# How to Decide: *Is This Person a Friend or Frenemy?*

First, it is vital to know the characteristics of a good friend and the characteristics of a bad friend. Have you heard the saying," birds of a feather flock together"? This saying is often used to encourage you to be mindful of whom you spend time with and remind you that your friends can lead you to success or failure.

Second, in choosing friends, accept that not everyone will choose to be your friend or be friendly with you initially or at all. This is not something to be worried about as you may have the same feeling about them too. You also do not have to spend the effort changing who you are to make anyone like you.

Third, when choosing your new friends, they may have different interests than some of your current friends. This is OK. It will mean that you will do some activities with one set of friends, and other things with your other friends.

Fourth, recognize that your friends can come from many different experiences and backgrounds. Having a diverse group of friends exposes you to valuable experiences across racial, religious, cultural, social, accessibility and economic perspectives. You can gain so much by opening yourself to sharing and learning from others who seem different from you on the surface.

How can you distinguish if someone is a good friend? Set your standards for the types of friends you want and the kind of friend you want to be.

# Activity #4

In the section below write in the qualities of a good friend and a bad friend ("frenemy")

**Good Friend/Bad Friend or "Frenemy" Qualities List:**

| Good Friend | Bad Friend (a.k.a "frenemy") |
|---|---|
| | |

As a member of any friendship group, your opinion is as valuable as any other friends in the group. Share your ideas and listen to those of your friends. When deciding on how to spend your time together, do what makes you feel comfortable. Be aware, however, that sometimes there will be disagreements among friends. Most conflicts are resolved by talking things out honestly and listening to the other friend's side. Developing a strong bond of friendship happens when friends talk through difficult times and learn how to relate to and forgive each other.

In developing and maintaining your friendships, please pay attention to what your friends say about you and others when they are in both a good mood and bad mood. It is good to say something right away your friends says or acts in a manner that upsets you. When something like this occurs, tell your friend, how it made you feel. If your friend apologizes and does not act in this way again, this is a sign of a good friendship based on respect and consideration. If your friend continues to say things that are hurtful to you or about you or others, think about whether this person is truly a friend. Remember that the qualities of a good friend will apply to you too. When you are in doubt about whether someone is treating you like a friend or a frenemy, or if you, have been behaving more like a frenemy, you can review your list on the qualities of a good friend or bad friend to be sure.

## Key Takeaway

Whether you are quiet and prefer to be on your own while you settle into your new surroundings or are outgoing and able to chat with everyone, you will find that other students feel the same way you do. Accept that it takes time to adjust to this new social environment as you begin to expand your friendship circle and learn about the activities you want to participate in and who you want to spend time with; remember that it takes time to be comfortable with this new social environment. You can always take the time to speak with your family about your friendships and your feelings, and you can choose to develop relationships when you are ready with other students as the school year progresses.

# Setbacks and Oppositions

# Setbacks and Oppositions

---

You won't have perfect days, and you may have some terrible days. It may seem unbearable, but you will learn to overcome adversities and build resilience with time and support. Because you are going to face opposition, and things are not always going to go your way. It is important to know that there is a resolution to every problem and help and support are available from those who love and care for you, namely your parents, family, teachers and friends. Below are some examples of situations that may come up and suggestions on how to deal with them.

# Bad Grades: *Back to the Drawing Board*

If you do not understand your schoolwork, do not put the time into studying, or procrastinate on your homework, this will lead to poor marks. The effort you put in is going to be reflected in the results. You can address the bad grades by changing your behaviour, getting the help you need, and doing your part.

In the early chapter on "Getting Good Grades," suggestions were noted on the tips to help you succeed in your schoolwork. You do not have to speak poorly of yourself because of your grades. Review these tips on how to get good grades and take action.

# No Invitation. *No Problem*

Remember that friends invite friends over to hang out. If you do not get an invitation, this can be very hurtful and make you feel bad about yourself. You mustn't take this as a personal comment on your value or make assumptions. Ask your friend why they did not include you. Give your friends a chance to explain. They may have thought that you were busy, would not have been interested, or that you no longer wanted to hang out because of your other activities. Perhaps they may be feeling hurt too.

Either way, ask and find out what is happening and do not make assumptions. Friendships are worth talking through. If you are satisfied with the explanation, then you can forgive and move on.

Be observant, and if this happens again, this may indicate something else in your friendship group. You can then consider hanging out with maybe one or two people or another group.

## Schoolwork Meltdown: *It's Just Too Much*

Take time to breathe. Step back and away for a few moments to calm yourself down. Realize that you can get through this moment. The work may seem voluminous and complex, but help is available. Instead of looking at the entirety of the problem, break it down into smaller pieces.

- Review the instructions and the details of the assignment.
- Contact a friend in your class to discuss the assignment.
- Check the internet to help with your understanding of what is being required.

- At the next opportunity, connect with your teacher and ask for additional guidance on the work.
- Break the work into smaller pieces
- Ask your parents or a family member for help
- With meltdowns, time away to get perspective helps more than you think. You can revisit the work and prioritize what you need to do to help you get organized and finish the task bit by bit.

# Misunderstood: *No One Gets Me*

There will also be moments when you feel alone, and no one understands your pain and what you are going through. This feeling may be because someone you love has done or said something that hurt you, or it could be when you have worked so hard only to be disappointed, or you and your parents have gotten into an argument.

It may seem that your family or friends don't understand what you are going through and that what concerns you so deeply is no big deal. When you get this feeling, seek out another family member, guidance counsellor, trusted friend or

access the many **online mental health supports** such as **KidsHelp phone**.
https://kidshelpphone.ca/

Please call: 1-800-668-6868

You will find that people care about you very much and are willing to listen and help if you give them a chance to do so.

# Critiques and Criticisms: *Bring Them On*

Yes, there will be times when others will criticize you. Cicely Tyson, the famous activist, actor and model, once remarked, "nobody would bother to beat you down if you were not a threat." This statement speaks to a great truth. When faced with criticism from bullies or others that is not justified, consider that the one who is mistreating you may have recognized that you are very talented and have exceptional skills and capabilities. The false criticism maybe envy or jealousy.

Though your immediate reaction, when faced with criticisms, might be to look down on yourself, take a few deep breaths. Depending on the nature of the criticism and the person doing the talking, it could distract you from focusing on your task and discourage you from moving forward. If the comment is from a person who cares for you, the information they share may help you improve and do better; give it some consideration.

While you are young, it is an excellent skill to learn to listen to what others say even though you disagree with them. Remember, you always have the choice to respond with your own opinion or not say anything at all. Learning how to calmly not take any action when you are upset by something someone has said is a way to demonstrate that you are growing in maturity. This is a tough skill to learn (many adults are still working on this) but practicing deep breaths and counting to ten can help.

## Key Takeaway

It is not the end as saddened, angry or hurt as you may feel during this time. Give yourself some time. You will learn that it takes time to adjust from being a grade 8 student in your elementary school to being a newbie in high school. But remember, it will not always be like this. As the little kid who went to school for the first time, when you were four or five, persevered every day and made friends, learned to write your name, do the math and make your way around elementary school, you can do the same for your high school experience.

Rely on the same traits that helped you get through the early years of elementary school and that you continued to develop as you got older. You can become braver, more responsible, more independent and open to experiencing new things. High school is the next arena to continue developing to adulthood, and you can do it.

# These Struggles Do Not Last: *Joy*

A **Joy List** is a list that you create that identifies the many things in life that bring you joy. It can be activities, memories, movies, music, food or people. The criteria for the Joy List are that it is personal to you. You do not have to explain the list to anyone; get permission for what is placed on the list, and best of all - it is timeless. Memories can be from many years ago or yesterday. When creating your Joy List, remember that when you think about the items they need to bring you joy (via a smile, laughter, tears of joy, or a sense of satisfaction). In addition, the items on the list can be something that you wish to happen and are future dated like taking a trip. Another benefit of a Joy List is that you can add to it any time.

The purpose of the Joy List is to bring us back to a moment of joy when we feel stressed to help us go back to being our brilliant, fabulous selves. It centres your mind in a positive direction and away from dwelling on negative thoughts. A Joy List can remind you of past situations where you were delighted, and this sensation can release healthy hormones that make you feel good about yourself.

# Activity #5

**Create your Joy List:**

- 
- 
- 
- 
- 
- 
- 
- 
- 
-

# Choices, Decisions, and Inner Knowing

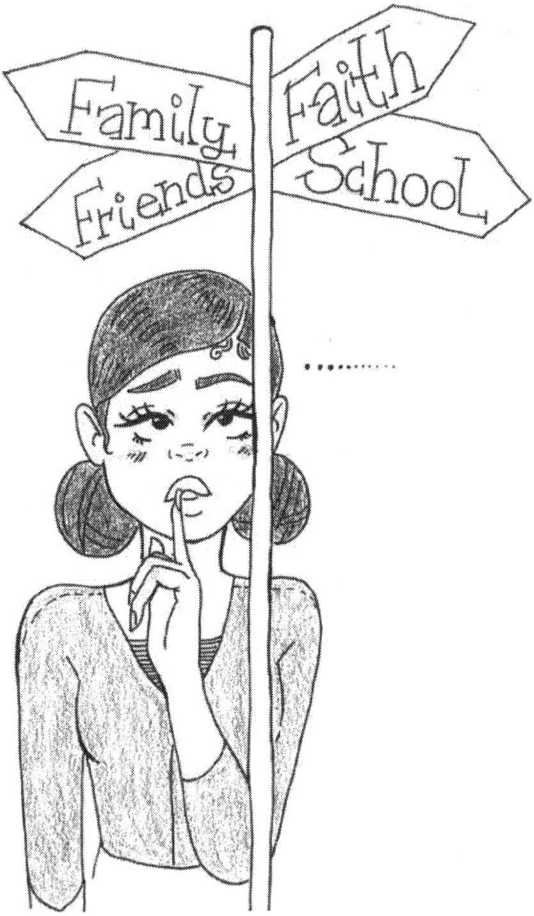
Family
Faith
Friends
School

# Choices, Decisions, and Inner Knowing

---

## Choices and Decisions: *What Is a Good Choice?*

In this section, let's spend some time thinking about decision-making and choices.

There are so many social activities that you will be exposed to during your high school years. These activities will require you to decide how to spend your time, money, energy, and emotions. The older you get, the more responsibility you will be given, including making choices that will demonstrate the type of person you are to your family, friends, teachers, and others you will encounter. Knowing how to make good decisions starts with having a good sense of what is of value to you.

For example, if you value family and keeping your commitments, you will keep your word and hang out with your little sister, even though you receive an invitation to go to the movies with friends.

If you value honesty and getting good grades, you will choose to put the time into studying and not copy off your friend's homework.

If you value friendship, you will stick up for your friend if someone says something negative about them when they are not around.

And when faced with choices that seem to be overwhelming and you just cannot figure out what to do, you will remember to consider the words from the "Talk" and the choice that will make you feel happy with yourself later.

# Making Decisions: *Why Am I Second Guessing?*

Has this ever happened to you? You need to make a choice, and after thinking about it for a while, you make a decision. After making the decision, another friend comments, and you start to second guess your decision.

Here are a few suggestions to reduce second guessing yourself:

**Step 1:** Set the criteria before deciding what it is you want to achieve.

**Step 2:** Be very clear on what you will not accept.

**Step 3:** Seek out the necessary resources and support and listen to objective feedback.

**Step 4**: Take the necessary action. Once you have reviewed the criteria and are satisfied that you have sufficient information, decide and follow through.

Making decisions after gathering the information you need is part of becoming more responsible and independent. As you begin to learn new things, ask questions, to help you sort your way through more minor decision-making challenges. You will gain confidence for the more significant and more exciting decisions you will make as you get older. Remember to be patient with yourself. Not every decision will lead to the outcome you want, but you can always learn from your decisions. When the decisions you make lead to the outcomes you wish, keep this in mind, too, as this is good information about what works well.

## Trust Your Instincts: *What's My Gut Telling Me?*

Another aspect of decision-making is learning to trust your instincts to keep you safe. There is a book called the *Gift of Fear* written by Gavin De Becker. In this book, he talks about the importance of not discounting your intuition when it speaks to you.

This intuition might show up as a feeling in your stomach or tingling at the back of your neck, to let you know that the person you are around or the situation you are in is not one of safety. When this feeling comes, please pay attention to it and remove yourself from the situation or the person's presence as soon as possible.

For example, you may be sitting on the bus, and an older male figure comes to sit beside you.
Although it may be difficult for you to do, if you are not comfortable, it is OK and a good idea to move to another position on the bus to feel safe. You should not stay in a place or with people if you are not feeling safe.

# What's My Exit Strategy: *I'm Out of Here*

Earlier, we talked about your travel route to and from school and why it is good to have alternate routes. Another critical aspect of staying safe is always being aware of your surroundings.

Whether it's getting home after a late practice or study session, being at a party, or walking down the street on your own or in a new neighbourhood, always be aware of who is present around you. If you are wearing earbuds or speaking on your phone, it is still essential to hear what is happening in front of and behind you.

Wherever you are, you must have a good sense of getting home at whatever time of day. Ensure that you always have the means to contact your family and can get home safely. Although it may take longer to get to where you are going, **the safer route is better.**

## Protecting What Is Private: *This Means More to Me than It Does to You*

There will be times when you may feel pressure to act in a certain way because of the crowd. You may be asked to do an activity to show that you fit in or have someone who wants you to do something to demonstrate that you like them. It might be a request to share personal private things about yourself. If you are ever in a situation where you are asked to share a revealing picture or a secret that a friend has shared with you, keep in mind that what is private to you is more important to you than to any other person you could share it with because it is yours. Some people will come into your life when you are sad and not feeling so good about yourself. At moments when you feel sad or upset, consider how you are being treated. Are you receiving words of encouragement to help make you feel better? If not, and the person you are with is saying things that are more hurtful or asking you to give them something personal at this time, be cautious. Remember the importance of choosing yourself over what might please someone else and make you unhappy. You do not have to give up anything of personal worth to you or place yourself in a compromising position, because you're sad in order to feel better. People who truly care about you would not ask you to do such things. Instead they will say kind words and do nice things to help build you up without asking anything of you in return.

Learn to trust your intuition to keep you safe. Choose to act in ways that are true to your values, no matter what.

# Activity #6

## What would you do if:

1. You enter the bathroom and hear another person crying in the stall beside you.
2. A friend texts asking you to join her to meet an older boy and his friends after school.
3. The person your friend likes sends you a message letting you know that he likes you.
4. One of your teachers makes you feel bad during class.
5. You are invited to two parties on the same weekend, and you have a test on Monday.
6. Your mom wants you to wear something that you think is totally out of style.
7. You hear some gossip about your friend that would hurt her.
8. You got a real high mark in class, but your other classmates did poorly.
9. You and your friend join an afterschool club together. After attending a few meetings, you like it, but your friend wants to drop out.
10. You are invited to a friend's house, and as you are about to leave for her place, she calls and cancels.

# Key Takeaway

Growing up includes making decisions about what matters to you. You will have more options and decisions to make in high school because your world has opened up. There will be trial and error as well as victories and triumphs in your choices. You can reflect on the outcomes of each option you take to help you make better choices in the future. One of the most important decisions of all is to decide to be true to yourself.

# The Awesomeness of You: *No One Else Can Do You*

_____

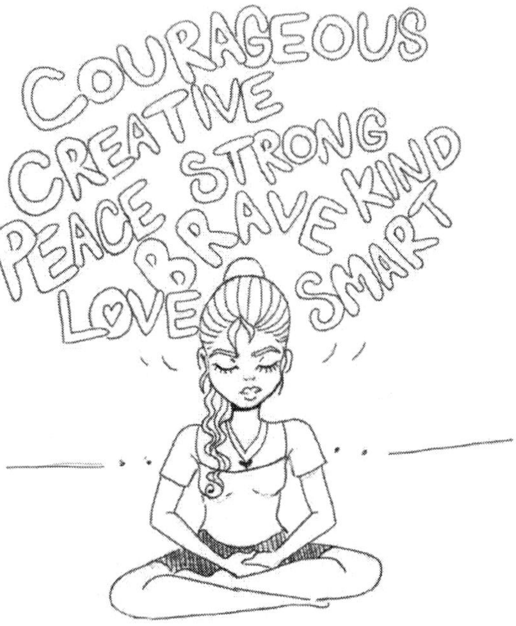
COURAGEOUS
CREATIVE
PEACE STRONG
BRAVE KIND
LOVE SMART

# The Awesomeness of You: *No One Else Can Do You*

---

## Talents and Gifts: *What Makes Me Unique?*

Although you are entering high school for the first time, you already have the potential to change the world and make it a better place because of your talents and skills. You may recognize your talents and gifts already. You might still be discovering your greatness.   But do know there is an awesomeness about being a girl.

There is a lot of evidence that girls are doing incredible things by simply doing what they love and enjoy making the world a better place. At age 9, Faith Dickinson made blankets to keep cancer patients warm. At age 11, Larissa Crawford fundraised to build a library. Malala Yousafzai, as a teen, promoted girls' education. At age 15, ballet dancer Yuan Yuan Tan, encouraged young dancers to follow their artistic dreams. At age 7, Jazz Jennings was one of the youngest transgender people to   be publicly documented, and continues to be an advocate for the transgender community today.

If you think back, you may recall the wonderful comments from your family when you were doing something that you enjoyed and did very well. Perhaps it was arguing with a brother or sister until you got your way, leading your friends in games on the playground or drawing characters and creating your own stories. Maybe you had a knack for making music or liked to design houses with items you found around the house.

As you grow older and are preparing for high school, you may think that these activities are childish, and now you need to set them aside. Well, you don't.

It might come about during your time in high school that you develop a deep passion for something new; it could be in the area of sports, arts, science, technology, writing, climate change, baking, performing, designing, politics or social justice. Or maybe a family member, teacher, guidance counsellor, or friend recognizes a talent or gift you overlooked in yourself.

You may not want to explore a particular talent or skill because you are concerned about other people's thoughts. When you are allowed to develop your abilities or skill further, you take the chance and go for it at school. You will find that there are more people for you along the way, including family members and teachers, who will gladly encourage and support you.

High school is a great time to learn to nurture your talents, build upon these abilities and explore untapped areas of creativity.

## Do Not Diminish Your Voice: *My Opinion Matters.*

In high school, students are very concerned about their reputation, what others think about them, how they look, dress, act, and speak. When you are navigating through your high school experience, it requires that you be courageous. Girls are judged by society on external factors, and they face pressure from friends, social media, and others. Changes are being made in the classroom and the wider world, but it is vital to grow in responsibility and independence to learn to speak up for yourself and others.

When you disagree with something, say so. When you are in support of something, say so as well. You will learn that when you act consistently with what you believe, this helps you build confidence, courage and increases your self-respect. Your voice and opinion matter, and when you share it, you will find that others will respect you more for doing so.

## Your Reputation and Personal Brand: *What's My Status?*

Reputation has been defined as what other people think or say about you, while character is defined as who you are. Reputation is the opinion of others based on what they may have heard or observed without any real understanding of your thoughts and feelings.

In high school, you might hear rumours about certain students described as tough, rude, cool, a bully, a diva, or a person with a criminal record. This reputation that some students have might be so well known that it inhibits their opportunity to be seen in any other perspective.

When you hear students speaking of other students you do not know, be mindful not to make assumptions based on rumours.

Consider this from your perspective, how do you want to be thought of by others? You are a whole person, and a reputation hardly captures what an individual is really like. As you get to know other students from other classes and different grade levels through the years, be open to getting to know who they are based on your interactions and not what others are saying.

The term "Personal Brand" is used quite a lot on social media, and the entertainment and music industry has made its way into how people talk about themselves. While it is good to associate your actions with positive images and products with a reputation for doing something with the environment or social justice movement, be mindful that you cannot be branded.

If you think to yourself that you are just average, think again. You are a unique individual, and no product, item of clothing, or association with a particular group can take away from the fact that you are fantastic just as you are. Picture a beautiful image from nature such as a sunset, rainbow, field of flowers or waterfall and consider that the

Creator who made that also made you; no branding required.

## Power of Words: *How Do I Describe Myself?*

Words significantly impact how we feel, what we think we can do, and our success. In high school and even now, you may notice how words are used to describe young girls. Because you are so important, you must pay special attention to the words you use and how you speak to yourself. As you continue through life, others will use words to describe you. It will be a good habit to practice saying kind and encouraging words to yourself every day.

Imagine that you are sitting in a place that brings you comfort. Picture a white envelope in front of you on the floor or the ground. As you open the envelope, notice that it is filled with Post-it® note sized square pieces of paper. Each paper is a bright fluorescent colour (pink, yellow, red, green, blue, purple). On each piece of paper is a word that describes you:

**"Brilliant, Fabulous, Kind, Awesome, Creative, Artistic, Talented, Bold, Strong, Brave, Adventurous, Spectacular, Musical, Athletic."**

What other positive words can be used to describe yourself? If you are not sure, ask a family member.

## Activity #7

**Words Matter.**

Take a few moments and write down a list of positive words to describe yourself. When you have done this, please put the words somewhere you can see them and read them **every day**.

# Be Confident: *How do I Get Some of That?*

When you are preparing to walk into a class, onto a sports field or enter a new space for the first time, do not think you belong.

At that moment, a host of insecurities may seem to come flooding over you. When you sense this unease after entering the environment, you may start to doubt your value, talents, and abilities. And you might even discount yourself because of your race, gender, identity, physical size, height, skin colour, accent, clothes, or beliefs. When this happens, take a few long deep breaths, hold your head up high and get hold of thoughts before they get away from you.

Remember to repeat positive words describing yourself, look around for a friendly face, and walk into that space. Do not be afraid of learning something new. You do not have to be fearful of walking into an unfamiliar setting in school. Take a few deep breaths to calm your nerves. Look around the room for a friendly face and put a smile on your face and in your heart. Think positively, that you can try out this new thing, and with confidence, walk right in and take a seat. And if you notice someone walking in after you, who seems afraid, share a smile with them and make room beside you.

# Spending Time with Family: *They've Got My Back*

Your relationship with your family will continue to be of great importance to you, and you will need to let them know that as well. There will be occasions when parents or relatives (younger and older) want to spend time with you, and it may seem that you are too busy or have other commitments. Relationships require effort, and the most important relationships can be taken for granted because we know our family's love is unconditional. Still, if you have siblings and other relatives in your life, spend time with them. Let them share with you their stories and time. You might find that this time is so special and brings you such happiness that it is worth declining invitations from friends to be with your loved ones.

A particular word about grandparents, if you have the blessing of a grandparent in your life, this relationship will give you more than you can imagine today and for years to come. The wisdom of grandparents and hearing about their life experiences can give you some of the best advice that you cannot find from any other individuals. Grandparents have an unbelievable perspective on the world and relationships. They have seen much, know much and are willing to hear what you have to say if you give them the time. Stay in touch with your grandparents and other relatives such as aunts and uncles if you are able, as they can all be an excellent support for you and connecting with them shows them that you care.

# Quiet Strength: *How Do I Become Confident?*

Look to your sacred scriptures for encouragement, hope, and direction for those who have a spiritual practice or belong to a particular faith. Spiritual practices give you a solid foundation upon which to set your beliefs and values. The time-tested truths of the faith can lead you to answers when you are confused or facing difficulties. Your family and others who share your faith will remind you of its teachings.

Attend a place of worship (Church, Gurudwara, Mosque, Temple, Synagogue). You can regularly participate in prayers, ceremonies, rituals, and practices that strengthen your faith to cope with and celebrate life circumstances.

Suppose you do not subscribe to particular faith practice. In that case, some high schools offer meditation and other mindfulness practices to assist students with lessening their anxiety and stress, increasing focus, solving problems, fostering discipline, managing emotions, and developing a positive outlook.

Seeking quiet and stillness is important for mental well-being to hear what is happening inside your heart and mind. The world of high school and its busyness can distract you from seeking stillness and re-setting. Quiet moments call you to listen, to reflect on how you are doing and help you adjust to the new environment.

When testing situations come, activities that strengthen your mind and sense of self will help you get through challenging moments and give you confidence for the days ahead. Listen to the voice and the words of those who love you. Remember, you know what is right; do the right thing even when it is not easy.

# Building Resilience: *I'm Ready for the Journey*

In the final section of this book, I would like to highlight that maintaining connections with your family, choosing good friends and being a good friend, doing your best at school and staying true to your values are ways to stay mentally well. To these actions, you can add eating healthy, getting the rest and sleep you need, doing things you love and having an optimistic view of life.

While healthy habits can be hard to keep up on your own, you and your friends can do this together. It's a "girl code" where you promise each other to stand firm together. You can be a source of unity, comfort and positivity for one another. When one of you is having a tough time, the others can rally around her and boost her up. When one of you excels, you can celebrate with each other. By the time you get to the conclusion of high school, you may find that your family group of girlfriends, teachers and all those you have met along the way will have made it an experience to remember.

## Key Takeaway

Before you know it, your first year of high school will be over. You will look back and ask yourself, why were you? As the year ends, you can reflect on the new friends you made, your ability to get around the school and understand the expectations of your teachers.

You may have joined a team or an afterschool club or even started a part-time job. Your family and teachers will be there for you for the continuation of this journey through high school. And next year, you can look out for the newbies who will be looking up to you to help them get through the first year.

# Conclusion

_____

# Conclusion

---

## *Less Catastrophic Than I Imagined*

At the end of my first year of high school, I still had pimples, but so did most of the faces at school. I had made a new set of friends, and we often laughed together while at our lockers, on our way to class and during class time. I worked hard on my schoolwork and most often completed my assignments at the last minute. I received good grades but needed to change some of my procrastination habits to do so, and I did in some subjects. I joined a few school teams and found many different routes to get to and from school. I would not say that I was by any means cool, but I

did my best to be kind and respectful. There were senior girls that I looked up to and older boys that I thought were absolutely gorgeous. My teachers were friendly and wanted me and my friends to do well.

My family was always there to support me and to give an encouraging word to steer me in the right

direction and remind me that "this too shall pass" when some other catastrophe blew into my life. I am thankful for the love that I received from my family consistently and unconditionally, and I could not have made it through without them. High school is a journey that teaches you so much about yourself, your friends and the world. So, are you ready?

# Activity #8

**Letter For Your Future Self.**

Take a blank piece of letter paper and write a short note to your future self. In the letter, describe yourself using positive words and images. This letter will remind you how awesome you are in times when you might have forgotten. Consider the following questions:

- What dreams do you have for yourself?

- What are the things that make you laugh?

- What activities do you enjoy doing?

- What are your gifts and talents?

- Go back to this letter in the upcoming years when you need encouragement or a reminder of how important and valuable you are.

# A Personal Note from the Author

---

Thank you for taking the time to read this book. There are many enjoyable experiences that you will have while in high school. Some of these experiences will be in the halls of your school; others will be out with your friends or while spending time with family. During these few short years, you may meet friends that will be with you and have your back for a lifetime.

Through your academic pursuits, personal relationships, and social interactions, you will also learn that there will be challenges and opportunities in all areas of your life. These will be good things because they will help you develop good judgement, help you think through problems and humble you to ask for and receive support. You will come to see that you can make a difference and more profoundly if you embrace the wonderful, brilliant and fantastic human being that you are and were created to be. No one can bring to this world what you have to give. Believe that you can and will pass through this part of your life's journey with so much love and support and will not be alone. Your ideas will be guided, and your acts of generosity and kindness towards others will reflect back onto you. As you prepare to go into the world and do great things, know that you are already perfect and divinely loved.

# In all things be strong, loving and fearless.

# Resources

Barrientos, S. (2021, January 29). "12 of Cicely Tyson's Most Powerful and Inspiring Quotes", *Goodhousekeeping Magazine*, Hearst Communications.

*Bologna, Caroline, (2019, February 26) Huffington Post, "16 Girls Who Changed The World Proof you're never too young to make an impact."* https://www.huffpost.com/entry/16-girlswho-changed-the-world_n_5a8f4f09e4b01e9e56b9e26c

De Becker, Gavin (1997) *The Gift of Fear: Survival Signals That Protect Us from Violence*. New York: Random House Publishing Group

Fox, Chris,(2021, May, 12) "TDSB to bring back 'quadmester' model for secondary students next year | CTV News." https://toronto.ctvnews.ca/tdsb-to-bring-backquadmester-model-for-secondary-students-nextyear-1.5425147

Haas, B. Susan (MD), (2012, April 23), *Psychology Today. "Why You Need a Joy List, Two simple exercises that could totally, joyfully, transform your life."* https://www.psychologytoday.com/us/blog/prescriptions-life/201204/why-you-need-joy-list

Kids Help Phone. "Kids Help Phone is always there for you. No matter what you want to talk about, we're here to listen. No judgment, totally private". https://kidshelpphone.ca/, please call 1800-668-6868.

Pirie, K (2015, April 28). *Real Simple Magazine.* "The Ultimate Self-Defense Guide We Hope You'll Never Need." Meredith Home Group

Rahmani, Tamara. *(2019, August), Canada Helps Blog. "16 Young Activists Changing the World."* https://www.canadahelps.org/en/giving-life/youthactivists-changing-the-world/#:~:text=%206%20Young%20Activists%20Changing%20the%20World%20,the%20way%20t hat%20transphobia%20and%20oppression...%20More%20

Smith, L. (2016, April 19) *No Fears, No Excuses, What you Need to Do to Have a Great Career.* Harper Collins Publishing LTD. Toronto

TED, (2009, March 26) "The difference between winning and succeeding John Wooden" (Video).https://youtu.be/0MM-psvqiG8

Tracy, B.(2007). *Eat That Frog!: 21 Great Ways to Stop Procrastinating and Get More Done in Less Time.* San Francisco, CA : Berrett-Koehler.

Toronto District Catholic School Board Program and Services (2021) Advanced Placement www.tcdsb.org/ProgramsServices/SchoolProgramsK12/AP/Pages/default.aspx

Toronto District School Board. (2014) High School Course Types TDSB https://www.tdsb.on.ca/HighSchool/Guidance/Course-Types

UC Berkeley School of Law. (2017, March 10 ) US Supreme Court Associate Justice Sonia Sotomayor at UC Berkeley (Video).https://youtu.be/etcWbvwv2iU

Wong, D.(2016, January 18), "How to Stop Procrastinating on Homework: 30 Powerful Tips That Work. "https://www.danielwong.com/2016/01/18/stop-procrastinating-onhomework/

Youth Central, (2018, March), "Top 10 Study Tips", https://www.youthcentral.vic.gov.au/studyand-training/help-with-study/how-to-studybetter/top-10-study-tips

# Acknowledgements

This book would not have come together without the love and encouragement from my mom Marcella Carasco. You listened thoroughly to all my stories and guided me during my high school years and even now. When I had doubts, you told me to trust in God and keep going.

For my dad Martin, you are away from me for now but always remain in my heart. Thanks for teaching me how to look anyone in the eye to protect and keep myself safe and choose the better route.

To my dear brother Marcus, you are the ideal big brother, strong, dedicated and always willing to do whatever it takes to protect me from harm and keep me safe. Thanks for having my back.

To my loving husband Keith, from the moment you took my hand, I knew you were a man of gentleness and quiet strength. You love me just as I am. Thanks for all your support.

To my niece Maia, whom I watched grow up with pride, confidence and concern for others, you inspired this book. To my nephew Malik, from the beginning, you brought me joy.

Thanks to my younger nieces and nephews, I hope you read this book one day and are encouraged to look forward to your high school days with excitement.

A special thanks to Lydia and my other aunts, my uncles and grandparents, who taught me many lessons and reminded me of our values.

Many thanks to my Book Doula, Andrea Seydel, who helped bring my book to life. Thank you for your patience and enthusiasm along the journey to getting my book published. Many thanks to Lindy Bailey for proofreading and editing my manuscript.

My teacher friends shared their knowledge of the high school system and their observations of the student experience.

Jade Brown, thank you for your wonderful illustrations. You agreed to help me out right away with this work, and your talent is exceptional.

I am deeply grateful to all the young girls who participated in the workshops and shared their stories prepared for high school. Your courage, openness, sense of humour and vulnerability in our sessions made me confident that the world will be better because of you.

Most importantly, I thank God, who loved me first, for all His love, grace and mercy.

# About the Author

**M**arcella was born on the Caribbean island of St. Lucia, and her family immigrated to Canada when she was a young child. She spent most of her elementary and high school years in Brampton, Ontario, Canada.

Marcella is a long-standing member of the Human Resources Professional Association (HRPA), and she holds the designation of a Certified Human Resources Leader (CHRL). She has a Certificate in Human Resources Management with other credentials, including a Bachelor of Arts Honours Degree.

Marcella is the founder of Marcella Kowalchuk Consulting Incorporated and provides human resources advice to leaders in the private, public and not-for-profit sectors.

Marcella engages with youth and young adults delivering workshops that help to prepare them for their transition to high school, post-secondary academic institutions and the working world. Through her work, Marcella is committed to inspiring others to go into the world to do great things in business, career and school.

This book is Marcella's humble effort to please God through this work, by sharing lessons on how to navigate the high school experience and in thanksgiving for all the graces received.

Marcella lives with her family in Ontario, Canada.

You can reach Marcella at
www.marcellakowalchukconsulting.ca

PUBLISHING

# Live Life Happy-Publishing

Helping people painlessly give birth to
books that change lives.

Dear Reader,
Thank you for purchasing this unique book and
joining the **Live Life Happy Community** of
readers. We are a publishing company that is
committed to bringing positive, supportive and well-
being-enhancing books to life.

As a welcoming gift, we'd like to offer you free
access to the **Live Life Happy Book Vault**, which
is full of resources and support to help you live a
flourishing life. You can gain access here:
www.andreaseydel.com.

Finally, If you or someone you know has been
thinking about writing a book, sharing a message or
gaining credibility in an industry, I can help you
painlessly give birth to your book. As a book doula
and founder of LLH Publishing, I help make author

***book-writing dreams come true***.  Best of all, these books are changing lives, and your message can help others too. So don't hesitate to reach out and set up a Book Chat, and please stay in touch!

Sincerely,
Andrea Seydel
(The Book Doula)

Questions? Comments?  Contact me at andrea.livelifehappy@gmail.com.

**P.S. Books Change Lives: Whose life will you touch with yours?**

Made in the USA
Columbia, SC
02 June 2022